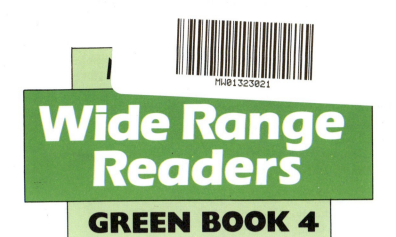

Wide Range Readers
GREEN BOOK 4

Fred J. Schonell
Phyllis Flowerdew

Oliver & Boyd

Acknowledgements
We are grateful to the following for supplying photographs and giving permission for their use: All-Sport, cover and pp. 128, 129, 132, 136, 141 (photos by Tony Duffy and Steve Powell); Colorsport, p. 130; Picturepoint, London, p 124; Syndication International, p. 100; ZEFA, p. 76.

Illustrated by Peter Cornwell, Terry Gabbey, Carol Holmes, Trevor Parkin and Barry Wilkinson.

Oliver & Boyd
Pearson Education Limited
Edinburgh Gate,
Harlow,
Essex CM20 2JE

An Imprint of Pearson Education Ltd

First published 1951
Second edition 1965
Third edition 1976
Fourth edition 1985
Thirty-fifth impression 2015

© Phyllis Flowerdew and the Executors of the late Sir
Fred J. Schonell 1965, 1985.
(Expect 'Daley Thompson' © Anne B. English 1985.)

All rights reserved; no part of this publication may be
reproduced, stored in a retrieval system, or transmitted in
any form or by any means, electronic, mechanical,
photocopying, recording, or otherwise without either the prior
written permission of the Publishers or a licence permitting
restricted copying issused by the Copyright Licensing Agency
Ltd, 90 Tottenham Court Road, London, W1P 0LP.

ISBN 978-0-05-003752-2

Set in 14/20pt Monophoto Plantin
Printed in China
SWTC/35

Preface

The Wide Range Readers are planned to provide graded reading practice for junior school children. Because children of 7–11 have a wide range of reading needs and attainments, there are three parallel series—Blue, Green and Red books—to provide plenty of material to suit the interests and reading ages of every child.

Books 1–4 are graded by half yearly reading ages, for use by appropriate groups within a class. Book 1 should provide an easy read for children with a reading age of about $7-7\frac{1}{2}$. Children with reading ages below 7 are recommended to use the Wide Range Starters.

The controlled vocabulary of the series makes the books suitable for the following reading ages:

$6\frac{1}{2}-7$	**Starter Books**—Blue, Green and Red
$7-7\frac{1}{2}$	**Book 1**—Blue, Green and Red
$7\frac{1}{2}-8$	**Book 2**—Blue, Green and Red
$8-8\frac{1}{2}$	**Book 3**—Blue, Green and Red
$8\frac{1}{2}-9$	**Book 4**—Blue, Green and Red
$9+$	**Book 5**—Blue, Green and Red
$10+$	**Book 6**—Blue, Green and Red
$11+$	**Book 7**—Red only
$12+$	**Book 8**—Red only

Contents

page

5	The Horse and Ann
22	The First Cart
35	The Travelling Dog
45	A Song for a King
54	Samson
76	Falling Leaves
78	Escape for Three
91	Kiri
102	The Boy who Loved Ships
110	Prairie Fire
123	The Olympic Games
132	Daley Thompson

The Horse and Ann

Ann wanted a horse. She had always wanted a horse. She lived in a country cottage which had a field as well as a garden. It even had an old stable at the side. It seemed to have everything Ann needed—except the horse.

Then one day, her wish came true. A letter came from her grandfather.

It said, "If you can meet me in town on Saturday at 10 o'clock, I'll take you to the horse fair and buy you a horse."

Ann could hardly believe it.

"Oh, Mum," she cried, "isn't it wonderful? Now I'll be able to ride like the children on the farm. I'll be able to ride every day."

Her parents were pleased too.

"It's very kind of Grandfather," they said.

"Oh, it's wonderful!" went on Ann, dancing up and down. "I'll choose a big brown horse with a glossy coat, and I'll teach him to carry me over the fields and the hills. I'll teach him to gallop like the wind."

There were only five days to wait until Saturday, but to Ann they were the longest days she had ever known. She thought Saturday would never come.

But of course it did. Then her mother and father took her to the bus stop and said,

"You'll be back for dinner, I expect. Now see that you choose a good horse."

"Oh, I will," replied Ann. "I'll choose a great big brown one with a glossy coat, and I'll teach him to gallop like the wind."

Just then the bus came. Ann climbed on to it, waved goodbye to her parents, and started on her journey.

When she reached town, there was Grandfather waiting at the bus stop, and in a few minutes they were at the horse fair together.

There were crowds of people moving to and fro, and there were many horses of different kinds. Most of the horses waited patiently while people looked at them and felt them, but some of them tossed their heads and gave loud, shrill sounds of anger or fear. Ann stood still in delight and excitement.

"Now," said Grandfather, "you may choose whichever horse you like. But remember that you want it for riding, so don't choose a cart horse."

"Oh, no," replied Ann. "I know just what I want. I want a big brown one with a glossy coat. I'll teach him to gallop like the wind."

Grandfather and Ann walked over to a line of riding horses. Ann looked from one to another.

"Oh, they're beautiful!" she exclaimed. She scarcely noticed black horses and grey horses, but she moved on slowly from one brown one to the next.

"They're all so beautiful," she murmured. "It'll be quite hard to choose the right one."

"Never mind," replied Grandfather. "There's plenty of time."

Slowly Ann walked up and down the line again. There were so many big, brown glossy horses that she didn't know which to choose. Any one of them would carry her over the fields and the hills. Any one of them would gallop like the wind.

"Look at the crowd of people over there," said Ann suddenly. "Let's just go and see what they're looking at." She pulled at Grandfather's hand and led him to the front of the crowd.

"Oh!" whispered Ann, for in a pen was a little foal. It was brown and slim, and stood uncertainly on long thin legs. It looked much too young and small to be away from its mother. It gave soft little cries of unhappiness, and pressed its nose against the coat of the man beside it.

"Its mother died," Ann heard the man say, "and I haven't time to look after it myself."

"It's a fine little horse," said someone else, "but I doubt if you'll sell it. Most farmers are too busy to mother such a young thing."

The foal moved a few steps, and its legs looked more awkward than ever. It raised its head, and looked round with frightened brown eyes.

"Oh, Grandfather," said Ann, "that's the horse I want. Please buy him for me."

"Oh, you can't have that one," said Grandfather, smiling.

"Oh, please," begged Ann. "That's the one I want!" Gone was her dream of a big brown horse with a glossy coat. Gone was her dream of galloping like the wind. She just wanted this poor little frightened foal. She wanted him more than anything in the whole world.

"But you won't be able to ride it for a long while," said Grandfather.

"I know," replied Ann. "But he'll soon grow, won't he?"

"Yes," agreed Grandfather, "he'll grow quickly enough."

He put his arm round Ann, and said,

"We'll go and look at the others again, shall we?"

"Oh, please buy me this one," begged Ann, nearly in tears. "He *must* have someone to look after him, and you said I could choose whichever I liked. Oh, *please*, Grandfather!"

Grandfather felt he ought to say "No" very firmly, but he had said Ann could choose, and he was very fond of Ann. So he said,

"Are you sure?"

Then he said, "All right," and paid the money, and the foal was Ann's!

The man who sold it agreed to take it to Ann's house in his lorry. He gave Ann a bottle of milk with a rubber teat on the top.

"It's the only way he'll drink yet," he explained, "but he has two meals of corn a day."

So very soon Ann was standing outside her

own house once more, holding the little foal on a rope, and watching the lorry drive away in a cloud of dust, taking Grandfather back to town with it.

At that moment her mother and father came to the door. They stared at Ann and the little foal. Then they both exclaimed,

"Ann! *That* isn't the horse you've bought, is it?"

"Y-es," replied Ann a little doubtfully.

"But you can't ride on *that*!" said her mother.

"Whatever was Grandfather thinking about, to let you have it?" her father exclaimed.

"He didn't really want me to have it," explained Ann, "but he'd promised that I could choose whichever one I wanted. And this one looked so small and frightened, and he needed someone to look after him! You see his mother died—and—and—"

"All right," said her mother gently. "Let's make him comfortable in the field. We can talk about him afterwards."

Later, at dinner time, she said,

"Ann, you know you won't be able to ride that little foal for a very long while, don't you?"

"Yes," said Ann.

"You won't be able to ride him for two years," added her father. "Two whole years!"

"Two—*years*?" whispered Ann.

She had known it would be a long time, but she had thought a long time meant a few months—or a year at the most. Two *years*! She was seven now—that meant she would be nine before she could go galloping over the hills. Two years! Her face went very pink.

"If you'd like to change him," said her father

kindly, "we'll take him back straight away, and buy you one that you *can* ride."

Ann said nothing.

"Would you like to do that?" her mother asked softly.

Ann gulped. Two whole years! And she wanted to ride so much! For a moment she almost thought she would say "yes." Then she suddenly caught sight of the little foal in the field outside. He stood uncertainly on his funny, long legs, and he looked up in wonder as a white butterfly flew past his nose.

"I don't mind about not riding," said Ann quickly. "I don't mind waiting, if you'll let me keep the little foal."

So of course she kept him.

She fed him with milk and corn. She put clean straw in his stable every evening, and led him into the field every day. She patted him and hugged him and talked to him—and sometimes when he cried at night she even put on a coat and crept out of bed to comfort him.

But he wasn't unhappy for long. How could he be, with someone who was so kind to him? He began to love Ann as much as she loved him. He followed her. He listened to her voice. He seemed to understand everything she said.

And of course two years passed at last—as years always do. By that time Ann was nine and the little foal was a big brown horse with a glossy coat. He was as beautiful a horse as anyone could wish to see, and he learned to carry Ann over fields and hills, and he learned to gallop like the wind.

The First Cart

Lok and Shan, the cave children, were swinging in the forest. Father had gone out hunting, and they had gone part of the way with him. Then they had stayed behind to play among the trees.

"Look at me," said Shan, swinging from one hand like a monkey. Lok sat on a higher branch and shook it, so that the air was filled with the sound of rustling leaves. Then he climbed further out and hung with his feet dangling just above Shan's hand.

"I can touch your hand with my toes," he cried.

Shan shrieked with laughter and held on quickly with the other hand.

At that moment a shout echoed through the trees. It came clearly to the children's ears, and then died away in echoes, each softer than the one before.

"That's Father calling," said Shan, jumping down to earth.

"He must have killed something," added Lok, swinging himself down beside her.

"I'll race you," he added. So the children gave an answering shout and hurried through the forest. When they couldn't pass because the bushes were too thick, they swung from branch to branch along the tree-top way.

Father called again many times, so that Lok and Shan could hear him and follow the sound of his voice.

"There he is!" said Shan after a while. "Oh, look!"

There in a clearing sat Father, sharpening his knife of flint. And there beside him on the grass lay the body of a huge deer.

"Roast deer for supper tonight," said Lok.

"It's big enough to feed the people in the other caves too," added Shan.

"Father, what a big one!" they cried as they ran up to him.

"Yes," replied Father. "It's so big and heavy that I can't even carry it home."

"We'll have to help," said Lok.

"No," answered Father. "It will be too heavy for you. You must stay here and look after it, while I hurry back to the caves and get Raff to help me. He's a strong man. We'll be able to sling it on a stick and carry it between us."

So Father hurried away through the forest, and the children stayed to look after the deer. At first they sat and talked, or just looked at the deer and thought what a good hunter Father was. Then they began to play along the sandy path near by.

Lok found a branch that had been broken down in a storm. It was strong and thick, and half-way down it curved and forked out in two. He dragged it along, and shouted to Shan to catch it. The forked branches made two tracks in the sand, and the leaves still clinging to it made a pleasant swishing sound.

"Catch it! Catch it!" cried Lok, running

along the path. Shan ran close behind, bending down, and stretching out her hands to catch it. At last she caught hold of a handful of the leaves, and made Lok stop.

Then it was her turn to run while Lok tried to catch the branches.

After a while, Lok said,

"Go slowly Shan, and let me stand on it." So Shan held the straight part like a handle, and Lok stood on the forked part, with one foot on each curved branch.

When Shan pulled it along the ground, Lok tried to keep his balance. He could stay on only for a few seconds, but he kept trying until he could ride for a little longer.

The time passed quickly while the children played their new game. Soon they were quite out of breath with laughing and balancing and falling; and they sat down beside the deer to rest again.

"Father is a long while," said Lok.

"Perhaps he can't find Raff," replied Shan.

"He's a *very* long time," said Lok when they had waited a little longer.

"I wish we could carry the deer ourselves," murmured Shan. "Then *we* could take it home."

"Mmm," agreed Lok. He leaned against the deer and was silent. Shan started threading red leaves on a thin stick, humming a little tune to herself.

Suddenly Lok said,

"I've an idea! I wonder if it would work."

"What is it?" asked Shan.

"If we were to tie the deer to the forked branch," replied Lok slowly, "we *might* be able to pull it along."

Shan jumped up at once and pulled the branch nearer.

"We could try," she said.

They cut a long twining stem from a plant, and used it to tie the deer's legs together. Then they put the ends of the forked branches close to the deer, and they held its legs, and rolled it over on to the curved part.

With more strong, twining stems they tied the deer's legs to the branch. Then Lok and Shan held the long handle part and pulled hard.

At first they couldn't move the deer.

"Pull harder," said Lok. They both pulled harder. Then suddenly the branches began to move. There was a rustle of leaves, and the swish of the forked branches as they slid along the sandy path. The branches were like the runners of a sledge, and once they had started moving they carried the deer quite easily.

"Keep pulling," cried Shan.

"It's quite easy, isn't it?" said Lok. "But we'll have to keep to the path."

So Lok and Shan walked on, pulling as they went, and the forked branches came steadily on with the deer, leaving two long tracks behind in the sand.

"It's a wonderful idea," said Lok.

"It's a cart," added Shan. "We've made the first cart."

So the two cave children pulled their cart along the path until they reached the cave.

There they saw Father and Raff, just setting out towards the forest.

"Look!" they shouted. "Look at our cart!"

They shouted, "Cart! Cart! Cart!" at the tops of their voices, until everyone came out of the caves to see. Mother came, with Small Baby on her back, and Baby clinging to her bearskin skirt.

"Roast deer for supper tonight," she said.

"Look!" shouted Shan. "Cart, cart, cart! We've made the first cart in all the world!" And of course they had!

  ★ ★ ★ ★ ★ ★

Many years later someone found that the cart would go more easily if slim tree trunks were put underneath for rollers.

Then hundreds and hundreds of years later still, someone else (perhaps another Lok and Shan) thought of cutting thick slices from a tree and making wheels, but that is another story altogether.

The Travelling Dog

It was midnight in Albany, a town in America. The streets were silent except for the flutter of one dry leaf and the pattering paw-steps of one stray dog.

He was a shabby little dog, with a short, rough coat and small floppy ears. He was thin and hungry and very cold; and he was looking for somewhere to shelter. Soon he saw a light a little way ahead. It came from the Post Office, where men were sorting the mail.

The little stray dog went up to the door and pushed it gently with his nose. Ah! It opened. He crept inside, and stood still a moment, blinking in the light.

"Hallo, old chap!" said a friendly voice. The dog looked up and saw a man with a bundle of letters in his hand. He walked across to him, wagging his tail.

"Hallo, old chap!" said the man again, bending down to pat him.

The dog wagged his tail harder than ever.

"He's a bit thin," said another man.

"He looks like a stray," said a third.

The dog went from one to another. He wagged his tail so hard, and looked up with such friendly brown eyes, that the men couldn't help liking him.

They gave him some tea in a saucer and they shared their sandwiches with him. The dog was very pleased. He lapped up every drop of tea that splashed over the saucer. He ate every crumb of bread that fell upon the floor. He wagged his tail, to say, "Thank you."

Then he curled up on a pile of mail bags and fell asleep.

The men went on sorting the mail, but

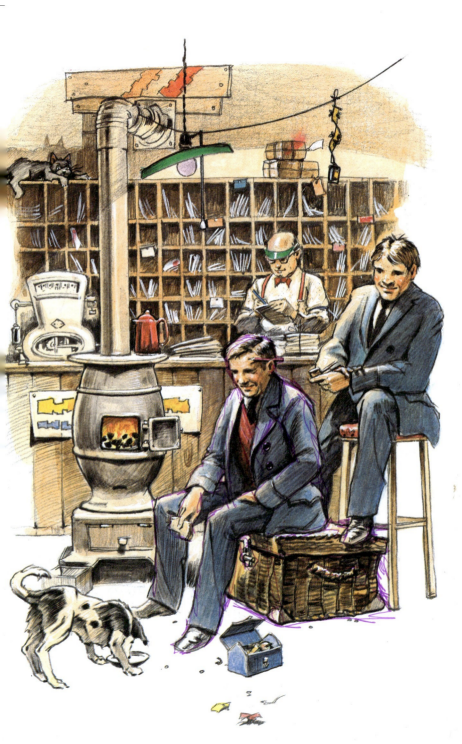

sometimes they looked across at the dog and smiled. For some reason they called him Owney, and Owney became the Albany Post Office dog.

He made friends with all the men who sorted the letters at night, and all the men who sorted the letters during the day. He made friends with the postmen who came and went in their vans.

There was always someone to pat him and play with him. There was always someone to say,

"Hallo, Owney. How are you today?"

And there was always a pile of warm mail bags to sleep on when he was tired.

So Owney was very happy. *He* was the Post Office dog!

One day a postman was loading his van with mail bags full of letters for New York. Owney stood at the van door and wagged his tail. He looked at the postman with friendly, brown eyes.

"Would you like to come with me?" asked the postman. "All right. Jump in."

So Owney jumped into the van and rode to New York with the mail bags. He must have enjoyed the ride very much. Or perhaps he thought he ought always to take the mail bags. Anyway, from that day, Owney became a travelling dog, and wherever the mail bags went, he went too.

When the mail bags went by van, Owney went by van. When the mail bags went by train, Owney went by train. He always saw the bags safely to their journey's end, and then went home again.

The men in the Post Office were afraid of losing him. So they bought him a collar and put his name and address on it. They also tied a little note to it asking railwaymen and postmen to fasten tags to his collar, saying where he had been.

Soon Owney was the friend and pet of hundreds of men; and there were so many labels and medals fixed to his collar that it wouldn't hold any more. Then a postmaster gave him a harness, and the new tags were fastened to that. All the postmen and railwaymen loved Owney. They were always pleased if he came to their station or post office.

So Owney went on travelling with the mail bags and wagging his tail all over America. Once more the collar and the harness became so heavy that the medals were taken off and put in a glass case in the Post Office at Albany. On one of these labels a verse was written:

"Only one Owney,
And this is he.
The dog is aloney,
So let him be!"

Other tags told the men that he had been to Alaska, Canada and Mexico.

After that Owney's journeys became longer still. One day he saw the mail bags carried on to

a ship, so on to the ship went Owney. The mail bags went to Japan, so Owney went to Japan too. The Japanese people were so interested in him that he was given a medal by the Emperor himself. Then he went to China where he was given more medals.

On and on he went, by boat and train and van, from one country to another, until at last he reached New York again. Then he went home to Albany.

That night the men at Albany Post Office were talking about him as they sorted the letters.

"He's been away a long time," said one man.

"Longer than ever before," said another.

"I hope he's safe," added a third.

At that moment the door was pushed open, and in walked a shabby little dog with a short rough coat and small floppy ears.

"Owney!" cried the men. "Dear old Owney!"

Owney wagged his tail, and came close, so that the men could look at all his new medals.

"Japan!" exclaimed one.

"China!" said another.

"Good gracious!" cried someone else. "He's been all round the world—round the world in 132 days!"

They petted him and patted him, and Owney was as pleased as could be. He had taken hundreds of mail bags. He had seen thousands of letters safely to their journey's end, and perhaps he knew that he was the greatest dog traveller in the world!

A Song for a King

Blondel sang. His voice echoed through the palace, and came to the ears of the soldiers who strolled in the courtyard.

"It's good to hear Blondel again," they said, and they stopped talking awhile to listen to his song.

It was Blondel's work to sing, for he was the palace minstrel, and one of the best singers in England, but today he sang because he was happy. He was happy because the first soldiers had returned from the Holy Wars. Soon others would come back, and with them, any day now, would come Richard the King. It seemed so

long since Richard had gone to the wars. Blondel had been ill at the time, or he would have gone too. But now Richard was on his way back. Soon he and Blondel would sing to each other—the new songs they had written and the old songs they had sung many times before—for not only was Richard the King, and Blondel his minstrel, but they were very great friends.

Suddenly Blondel stopped singing, for he heard horses' hooves beating on the stony road. He looked out of the window, and saw more soldiers returning. Their clothes were shabby and their banners were tattered. Perhaps Richard was among them. Quickly Blondel ran to meet them, calling a welcome, looking from one to the other. Richard the King wasn't there.

"Tell me," said Blondel, when he had greeted them all, "how is King Richard?"

"He was well when last we saw him," replied one of the soldiers. "We came back in small parties because it was not easy to travel across Europe. The King said he would follow. He will be here any week now. Sing for us Blondel. It is a long time since we heard your voice, and the songs of England."

So Blondel sang.

But the weeks went by and still Richard didn't come. Weeks turned to months and still he didn't come. Blondel's happiness changed to sadness, and his hope to despair.

"Perhaps the King is ill," he thought. "Perhaps he's been killed somewhere in Europe." He sang no more now, except to please the people in the palace. Day by day, week by week, month by month he waited for Richard.

Then at last news came. A weary soldier, limping to the palace one evening, brought a message that Richard had been captured on his way back from the Holy Land. He had been imprisoned in a castle somewhere in Europe, but even the weary soldier didn't know where.

That night Blondel lay awake, thinking of Richard. There were many countries in

Europe. Richard might be in any one of them. There were hundreds of castles in Europe. How could he know in which one Richard was imprisoned?

"I'll sing," thought Blondel. "I'll sing outside every castle in Europe, until Richard hears me, and answers."

Next morning he took food and money, and rode to the coast. There he sold his horse, and joined a ship going across the Channel to

France. Then the search began.

He had not walked far before he came to a castle. He stood outside and sang as loudly as he could. He sang the old songs that Richard knew, and he listened anxiously for Richard's answering voice, but it didn't come.

"I could hardly expect to be right first time," he said to himself, and he walked on along the winding road.

At first he found it pleasant to sing at castles, for he was often invited in, to sing to dukes and princes. They admired his fine clothes and

velvet cloak, and though they couldn't all understand his language, they were full of praise for his songs, and they paid him well.

So Blondel's voice echoed and echoed through the castles of France. Day after day, in different towns and villages he sang English songs, the old songs that Richard knew. Day after day he listened anxiously for Richard's answering voice, but it didn't come.

Soon he grew shabby. His clothes became worn and dusty, and his velvet cloak became tattered and torn. He was too shabby now to sing to dukes and princes. He could make only a little money, by singing to their servants in the kitchens. Sometimes he felt so tired and sad that he almost gave up hope. Then he thought of Richard, waiting, hoping all these months to be set free.

"If it takes me twenty years," thought Blondel, "I'll go on singing till I find my King. Even if I have to sing outside every castle in Europe, still I'll go on till I find him."

So Blondel wandered over Europe, singing, singing, singing.

At last he came to Austria, where the mountains were tipped with snow, and where dark green pine forests spread down to the shores of shining lakes. The wild beauty of it gave new hope to Blondel and his voice sounded all the sweeter in the clear mountain air. So through Austria he went, singing, singing, singing.

One day he came to a valley, where the River Danube flowed wide and deep, and a castle stood on a rocky mountain-side. Up the steep path climbed Blondel, till he came to the castle. He looked down at the Danube shining through the trees, and he looked up at the rugged walls of the castle.

"Oh, Richard, Richard," he murmured. "If only I could find you—my friend, my King." Then he sang, as he had sung so many times before—so many, many times now. He sang an English song, an old song that Richard had

always liked best of all. His voice echoed down in the valley and up on the mountain-side and in to the castle. He sang two verses, and then waited.

A twig cracked beneath his feet and the wind stirred in the pine trees. Then there came an answering voice—an English voice, singing the next verse of the song.

"Oh!" breathed Blondel, and he fell on his knees to listen. Loudly the voice came to him—

the voice of his friend, Richard the King. At last, he had found the King.

With a voice that trembled with excitement, Blondel sang again, so that Richard would know that he had heard him. Then he turned and hurried back to England to fetch men and money to free the King.

★ ★ ★ ★ ★ ★

So, a few weeks later, King Richard was brought at last to England, back to his own palace. And there once more Blondel sang to him the old songs that he loved. Blondel's voice echoed through the palace, clearly, sweetly, and to Richard the King it was the most beautiful sound on earth.

Samson

Long ago in the land of Israel there lived a boy called Samson. He was tall and brave, and very strong. He was stronger than the other boys who played with him. He was stronger than boys much older than himself. He was stronger even than his own father, and the secret of his strength was in his hair.

In those days men and boys wore their hair

long, and didn't cut it very often, but Samson's hair was never cut at all. Once in the hot weather he had said to his mother,

"Let me cut my hair shorter while the days are so hot."

Then his mother had gone to the door to make sure that no one was passing, and she had said softly,

"Samson, you are very strong, and your strength is in your hair. If we were to cut your hair, you would be as weak as any other boy."

So Samson always remembered the secret that his mother had told him, and he never, never cut his hair.

Now the Israelites were at war with the Philistines, and they longed to drive them away, and live in peace again. The people of Israel often looked at Samson and thought to themselves,

"How fine it will be when Samson is old enough to be a soldier. Then we'll be able to beat the Philistines."

When Samson grew up, he did become a soldier, and he fought for the Israelites. He was so strong that the Philistines were all afraid of him, and they made a plan to capture him. But when they caught hold of him, six men at once, he just pushed them away.

When they bound him with ropes, he just stretched his arms and broke the ropes. When they locked him inside their city gates, he just lifted up the gates, gateposts and all, and walked out with them on his back.

Then the Philistines said,

"We must think of something else. We must find out the secret of Samson's strength so that we can capture him."

But the only people who knew the secret of his strength were his father and mother, and Samson himself, and they didn't tell.

Now about this time, Samson said to his mother and father,

"I'd like to get married."

"That will be very nice," replied his mother. "Whom will you marry?"

"Her name is Delilah," answered Samson. "She's a Philistine."

"Are there not enough women in Israel?" asked his father. "Can't you choose one of those instead of taking a Philistine woman?"

But Samson wanted Delilah. So he married her and they lived together happily for a long time.

Then one day, when Samson was out, some of the Philistines came to Delilah and said,

"Delilah, why is Samson so strong?"

"I don't know," answered Delilah. "I've never thought about it."

"If you'll find out for us," said the Philistines, "we'll each give you eleven hundred pieces of silver."

"Oh," murmured Delilah. It sounded such a lot of money. She would be able to buy all sorts of beautiful things with it. So that evening, when Samson came home, she said,

"Samson, why are you so strong? What could we do to make you as weak as any other person?"

"It's a secret," replied Samson.

"Oh, tell me," begged Delilah.

For a long time he wouldn't tell her. Then he said,

"All right. I'll tell you. If you were to take seven green twigs that have never been used by anyone, and if you were to bind me with them, then I should be as weak as any other person."

"Oh, is *that* the secret?" murmured Delilah. Then she sang softly to Samson; and because he was tired after his day's work, he fell asleep.

Then Delilah crept out and found seven green twigs that had never been used by anyone. She twisted them and tied them round Samson, but Samson went on sleeping.

Now some of the Philistines were hiding behind the curtain. When they saw that Samson was tied up, they crept out to take him prisoner.

"Samson, Samson!" cried Delilah. "The Philistines are upon you!"

Samson awoke at once and blinked his eyes. He felt the seven green twigs twisted round him. He saw the Philistines bending over him. He stood up and stretched his arms, and the seven green twigs broke as if they had been cotton. The Philistines had to hurry away before Samson took *them* prisoner.

A few days passed by, and then Delilah said again,

"Samson, why are you so strong? What could we do to make you as weak as any other person?"

"It's a secret," replied Samson.

"Oh, tell me," begged Delilah.

For a long time Samson wouldn't tell her. Then he said,

"All right. I'll tell you. If you were to take seven new ropes that have never been used by anyone, and you were to tie them tightly round me, then I'd be as weak as any other person."

"Oh, is *that* the secret?" murmured Delilah. Then she sang softly to Samson; and because he was tired after his day's work, he fell asleep.

Then Delilah crept out, and found seven new ropes that had never been used by anyone. She twisted them round Samson and tied them in many knots, but Samson went on sleeping.

Now again some of the Philistines were hiding behind the curtain. When they saw that

Samson was tied up, they crept out to take him prisoner.

"Samson, Samson!" cried Delilah. "The Philistines are upon you!"

Samson awoke at once and blinked his eyes. He felt the ropes tied round him. He saw the Philistines bending over him. He stood up and stretched his arms, and the seven new ropes broke as if they had been cotton. Then the Philistines had to hurry away before he took *them* prisoner.

Once more, a few days passed. Then Delilah said again,

"Samson, why are you so strong? What could we do to make you as weak as any other person?"

"It's a secret," replied Samson.

"Oh, tell me," begged Delilah.

For a long time Samson wouldn't tell her. Then he said,

"All right. I'll tell you. If you were to take a loom for weaving and weave my hair in it then I'd be as weak as any other person."

"Oh, is *that* the secret?" murmured Delilah. Then she sang softly to Samson; and because he was tired after his day's work, he fell asleep.

Then Delilah took the loom and wove his hair so that it was caught in the threads of the loom, but Samson went on sleeping.

Now some of the Philistines were hiding behind the curtain. When they saw that Samson's hair was caught in the loom, they crept out to take him prisoner.

"Samson, Samson!" cried Delilah. "The Philistines are upon you!"

Samson awoke at once and rubbed his eyes. He felt his hair caught in the threads of the loom. He saw the Philistines bending over him. He stood up and shook his hair, and down fell the loom with a crash. Then the Philistines had to hurry away before Samson took *them* prisoner.

For a few days after this Delilah did not worry Samson. Then she thought of the pieces of silver that the Philistines would give her if she found out the secret. So she said to him again,

"Samson, why are you so strong? What could we do to make you as weak as any other person?"

"It's a secret," replied Samson.

"Oh, tell me," begged Delilah.

"No," said Samson.

"Please tell me," said Delilah. "Three times you have teased me. Now tell me the truth."

"No," replied Samson.

Samson and Delilah were no longer happy

together, for every day Delilah asked the secret of Samson's strength. As soon as he awoke in the morning, she said,

"Samson, why are you so strong?"

As soon as he came home in the evening, she said,

"Samson, tell me why you are so strong."

And before he fell asleep at night, she asked him yet again,

"Samson, what could we do to make you as weak as any other person?"

She worried him and worried him each and every day. She worried him so much that at last Samson said,

"All right. I'll tell you. The secret of my strength is in my hair. If you were to cut my hair, I'd be as weak as any other person."

"Oh, is *that* the secret?" murmured Delilah, and this time she was sure that he had told her the truth. Then she sang softly to Samson; and because he was tired after his day's work, he fell asleep.

Then Delilah took a knife and she cut Samson's hair. The hair fell down on the floor, and lay there, dark and shining, but Samson went on sleeping.

Now the Philistines were hiding again behind the curtain. When they saw that Samson's hair was cut, they crept out to take him prisoner.

"Samson, Samson!" cried Delilah. "The Philistines are upon you!"

Samson awoke at once and rubbed his eyes. He saw the Philistines bending over him. He stood up and tried to push them away, but he couldn't do it, for he was as weak as any other person.

What had happened? What had happened? Why did he feel so weak and strange? Where had his strength gone?

Then Samson saw his own hair lying, dark and shining, on the floor. Then he knew that his secret had been told. His hair had been cut, and he was as weak as any other person.

  ★ ★ ★ ★ ★ ★

Then a sad time came for Samson. The Philistines cruelly blinded him, and put him in a small, dark prison. They put chains around his feet, and they bolted the iron door.

Samson tried to break the chains, but his

strength had gone. He tried to push down the iron door, but he was as weak as any other person.

Sometimes the Philistines brought him news of the war. The news was always the same. The Israelites were missing him. They were losing battles day after day. They were being beaten by the Philistines.

"Oh," thought Samson sadly, "if only I hadn't told my secret! If I hadn't told my secret, I could have saved my people from the Philistines."

One day the Philistines won a great battle. It was the fiercest battle they had fought, and they were filled with pride because they had won.

"Let's have a feast," they said, "because we're so happy."

So nearly all the Philistine soldiers met together in the largest hall in their city. It was a fine hall, with a high roof held up by posts of stone. The soldiers ate and drank a lot, and were full of merriment and pride.

"Now that Samson is in prison," they said, "we're winning every battle. In a few more days, all the land of Israel will belong to us."

Suddenly the Philistines thought of bringing Samson in to the feast. They wanted to gaze upon him and tease him about his strength. So they sent a soldier to bring him from the prison house.

Now Samson was ill and blind. So the Philistines told a little boy to lead him. The boy led him to the middle of the hall and the Philistines laughed and shouted.

"Come Samson!" they cried. "Show us your strength now."

But Samson knew he could do nothing, for he was as weak as any other person. Then he said to the boy,

"Please lead me to the two great posts that are in the middle, so that I may lean upon them."

The boy did as he was asked, and Samson stretched out his hands to feel the two great posts that held up the roof.

"Come Samson," cried the Philistines. "Show us your strength."

"Oh," thought Samson sadly, "nearly all the Philistine soldiers are here under one roof. If only I could save my people from them!"

Slowly he put his hand up to his hair. It had been growing in prison. It was getting long. Perhaps—perhaps—. Then Samson prayed.

"Oh, God," he whispered, "please give me back my strength just for one minute, so that I may save my people."

"Samson," called the Philistines again, "show us your strength!"

Then Samson stretched out his hands and felt the two great posts. He felt one with his

right hand, and one with his left hand. Then he pushed with all his might, and in that moment his prayer was answered and his strength came back to him!

He pushed—and the great posts cracked, and shivered and fell; and the great roof came crashing down upon the Philistines. So the Philistine soldiers were killed, and Samson died too. But Samson's work was finished, for he had saved the Israelites from their enemies.

Falling Leaves

In autumn when the leaves are turning brown and yellow, and whirling through the air, have you ever wondered why they do it? Why do they change colour every year? Why is the tree left bare all through the winter?

It happens like this.

When you are hot sometimes, you notice tiny drops of water on your face.

In the same way, leaves let out tiny drops of water most of the time. Now this is all right in the summer, when there is plenty of rain—for the roots can take in enough to make up for the water the leaves are losing.

But in the winter the ground is often hard with frost. The roots cannot find enough water, and the tree has to live on what it has stored. It seems almost as if the tree says to itself,

"I must drop my leaves before they give away any more of my water."

So in autumn the tree takes back from the leaves all the juices that are useful to it. The juices (some of which make the green colour) run through the veins, back through the leaf stem and into the branches.

The leaves are then left yellow or brown or red. The tree makes a little layer of cork across the place where each leaf stem joins a branch. This keeps the juices safely inside and makes it easy for the leaves to blow away in the next wind.

So there they go every autumn—brown and yellow—whirling through the air. And the tree holds its bare branches in lacy patterns against the sky—and keeps alive through the winter on the water it has saved.

Escape for Three

Long ago, in the city of Paris, three children sat at home by the fire. It was beginning to get dark, but they did not dare to light the candles, for the street outside was filled with noisy, shouting people.

"They sound so rough, and angry," murmured Jeanne, who was eight.

"I'm frightened," whispered Pierre, who was only five. "I wish Mother and Father would come."

"I hope they'll *not* come," said Robert anxiously. He was nine, and he knew that it would not be safe for Mother and Father to try to get home through the angry crowds.

"It will be much better for them to stay away until the trouble is over," he explained. "They know that Marie will look after us."

"I don't understand what the trouble is about," said Jeanne.

"Well," replied Robert. "It's like a war between the rich and the poor. There are many people in Paris who are so poor that they haven't enough money for food. So they have started to rob the rich people. They are turning them out of their houses and putting them in prison."

"Even the children?" asked Pierre.

"Yes, even the children."

Jeanne gazed round thoughtfully at the room in which they sat. It had beautiful soft chairs and couches. It had curtains of velvet, and tall, slim candles in stands of crystal and gold. She looked at her two brothers, so handsome in their fine clothes; and she looked down at her own dress, reaching to her toes in a cloud of pink frills.

"I suppose *we* are rich," she said.

"Oh, yes," replied Robert. "We're very rich. At present I wish that we were not."

Jeanne opened her mouth to say,

"Well, it isn't our fault." But at that moment the shouting outside became so loud that she covered her ears and crept closer to the fire.

Then the door opened, and in came Marie. Marie was the children's nurse and they knew that she would look after them whatever happened.

"Listen," she said softly. "We must leave Paris tonight. I'll take you to my brother's

farm, but the journey will be dangerous and I'll have to hide you. Put on your warmest cloaks and go down to the courtyard door, but don't open it until I come. I'll dress myself as an old farm woman, and I'll take you out of Paris in a cart. You will have to lie quite still, and let me cover you with straw. It will be uncomfortable, but you must be brave."

"Oh, we'll be brave," said Jeanne quickly, going out to fetch the cloaks. Pierre looked puzzled and rather frightened.

"It will be like a game of hide and seek," said Robert with a smile. "Real hide and seek. You'll play, won't you, Pierre?"

Marie hurried away, and Jeanne came in with the cloaks. They were thick and warm and cosy.

Robert felt very big. He was the eldest. He would have to look after Jeanne and Pierre.

"Remember," he said, "we'll have to keep quite still and not say a word. You'll be able to do that, won't you, Jeanne?"

"Yes," replied Jeanne.

"And you, Pierre?"

"Yes," said Pierre.

They fastened on their cloaks and went down to the courtyard door. It was quite dark now.

"I wonder where Marie is," whispered Pierre. Then the door opened, and there stood an old woman in a ragged black gown and a short tattered cloak. Her face was dirty, and some of her teeth were missing. Surely it couldn't be Marie! For a moment even Robert felt doubtful. Then the old woman put her finger to her lips and smiled; and the children knew it *was* Marie.

There was a horse outside the door with a small, open cart filled with straw. Silently Marie helped the children into the cart. They lay down on the hard boards, and let her put two sacks of vegetables beside them. They closed their eyes while she covered them with straw.

Then they heard her climb up in front and tell the horse to start. They heard the clatter of the horse's hooves in the courtyard and then they felt the jog, jog, jogging of the cart. The journey had begun.

Robert wished he could see the way they were going. He guessed Marie must be going the quietest way, where the crowds would not be so great. He wondered how long it would be before it would be safe to live in Paris again.

Jeanne thought about the poor people who had become so angry with the rich. She remembered the thin, ragged children she had sometimes seen in the city. She had never thought that they might be hungry.

Pierre thought how queer Marie had looked. Even some of her teeth were missing. Had she pulled them out?

Jog, jog, jog went the cart, over the cobbled streets. Sometimes the noise of the crowd sounded far away. Sometimes it seemed very loud and near, and once the children felt the cart stop. They heard a rough voice asking questions, and they heard Marie answering in a

strange voice like an old woman. Then they felt the jog, jog, jog starting again, and they sighed with relief beneath the straw.

Robert suddenly wondered what would happen when they reached the city gates. There would be men on guard there. They might search the cart. What would happen then?

Jeanne started thinking of Mother and Father, and wondering where they were.

Pierre had thought for a long while about Marie's teeth, but now he had fallen asleep.

Soon the cart reached the city gate, and a

guard's voice cried, "Halt!"

Marie pulled the reins, and the horse stopped.

"Where are you going?" asked someone loudly.

"Back to my son's farm," replied Marie in the trembling voice of an old woman.

The children heard footsteps as the guard walked to the side of the cart. Robert lay quite still, with straw pricking his face. Jeanne lay quite still, hardly daring to breathe. Pierre lay quite still, because he was asleep.

"What's in this cart?" asked the guard.

"Just a few vegetables I couldn't sell in Paris," replied Marie.

"Oh, we'll soon see if that's true," said the guard, and he reached up, and pushed his hand among the straw. He touched Pierre. Pierre was asleep. He touched Robert. Robert didn't move. He touched a sack of vegetables and pulled it up a little so that he could see in the top.

"All right," he said. "Take your vegetables home, old lady."

Marie pulled at the reins, and the horse trotted on again. Robert and Jeanne were quite stiff with lying so still. They wanted to stretch themselves and push the straw from their faces, but they did not move. Marie would tell them when it was safe. Jog, jog, jog went the cart. The noise of the town was left behind, and there was only the sound of the horse's hooves on the quiet country road.

Robert smiled to himself because the guard

had touched him, and thought he had been a sack of vegetables. He was longing to tell Jeanne about it.

Jeanne wondered if the angry, poor people had broken into the house in Paris. How glad she felt to be away from the noise and the danger! Pierre turned over in his sleep, and the straw rustled in the cart.

The journey seemed so long. *When* would it be safe to sit up and breathe freely?

At last the cart stopped again, and Marie leaned over and brushed the straw from the children's faces.

"You are dear, good children to lie so still," she whispered. "We're far from the city now, and the danger is over, but I think you'd better stay flat as you are—just in case."

Robert and Jeanne smiled up at her in the darkness. It was nice to be able to breathe freely again.

The sky was black like velvet. There were hundreds of stars shining like the candles in the

Paris house. Jog, jog, jog went the cart; and the children slept and woke through the silent night.

Then at last they saw the lights of a farmhouse. They heard voices, and saw people and a swinging lantern. One of the men must be Marie's brother—but one was Father, and there was Mother beside him!

"Mother, Father!" cried the children. "How

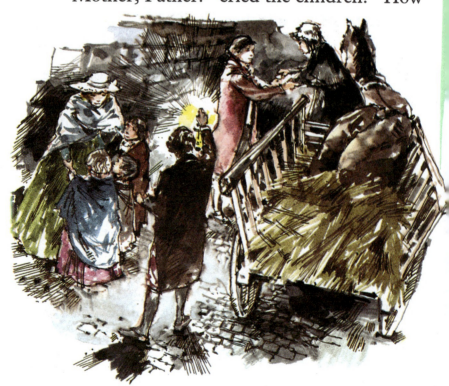

did *you* get here?"

"It wasn't safe to go back to Paris," explained Father, "and we guessed Marie would bring you here. Dear, good, brave Marie!"

"Father," said Robert, as he climbed out of the cart, "the guard at the city gate touched me through the straw, and he thought I was a sack of vegetables."

"Mother," said Jeanne, stretching herself at last, "when we go back to Paris, I want to give some of my dresses to the poor, ragged children in the streets."

"Marie," murmured little Pierre sleepily as Marie lifted him down, "what have you done to your teeth?"

"I've stuck black paper on them," she replied. "It's very uncomfortable, but I'll be able to take it off now."

So the children went into the farmhouse, blinking in the lantern light.

They all sat round the table, drinking hot

milk that Marie's brother gave them. Mother and Father looked at the children. They were dirty and untidy. Their hair was rough, and still had pieces of straw sticking in it. The boys' clothes were crumpled and creased, and Jeanne's pink, frilly dress was torn.

"Well, you don't look like rich children now," laughed Mother.

"In fact, you look very poor," added Father.

"Well, you can't expect *me* to look smart," said Robert. "I'm supposed to be a sack of vegetables."

"As long we're safe," remarked Jeanne, "I don't care whether we're rich or poor. Do you, Pierre?"

But Pierre's tousled head had dropped forward on to the table, and he was fast asleep again.

Kiri

Nell and Tom were New Zealanders. Nell's family had come from Britain long before, but Tom was a Maori whose people had been in New Zealand for hundreds of years.

Nell and Tom were hoping to adopt a baby. Their name had been on a list for some time, and now at last a social worker had arrived at the house with a baby for them to see. It was just five weeks old.

"Isn't he lovely?" said Nell, looking at the creased-up little face and the soft, dark hair.

"It's a girl," said the social worker.

"Oh." Nell's heart sank. "We asked for a boy," she said.

"Yes, I know, but there don't seem to be many about at present, and we thought if you saw this little girl you might change your mind."

Nell did not really mind whether she had a boy or a girl, but she knew that Tom had set his heart on a boy, so she said firmly,

"No. It's a boy we want." All the same she felt sad and troubled when the baby was taken away.

A few days later, the social worker called again, bringing the same baby.

"Oh, she's so sweet," said Nell. "Is she a Maori?"

"She's just what a child of your own would be," replied the social worker. "Her mother's family came from Britain, and her father is a Maori. It's very sad that they can't keep her themselves."

"Poor little thing," said Tom, "needing a good home and not finding anyone to adopt her."

Nell looked at him. *He* was the one who wanted a boy.

"Well, it's for you to say, Tom," she answered, and Tom of course said, "Yes."

So the baby came into their home, and they called her Kiri, a Maori word meaning "bell".

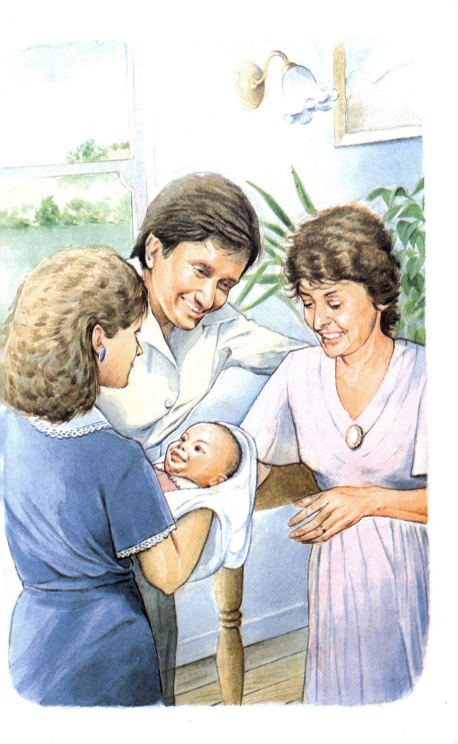

They had a big house with a number of spare rooms which they let to students, so there were always lively young people going in and out, and joining often in sing-songs round Nell's piano.

Nell had a great-uncle who had been a famous composer in Britain, and she often thought how nice it would be if little Kiri turned out to be musical. She might play the piano or violin or cello, or perhaps she might sing.

Meanwhile Kiri grew into a happy little girl with dark, wavy hair and big, brown eyes. She made lots of friends, and took part in little shows and concerts, dancing and singing, always helped and pushed forward by Nell. To Nell's great joy, it really did seem as if her little adopted daughter had a very good voice.

"Kiri," she would sometimes say, "some visitors are coming this evening, and I want you to sing to them."

"Oh no, I don't want to," Kiri would answer,

for she was a bit lazy, and would rather have played in the sunshine with her friends.

"Kiri," her mother would then add sternly, "you've been given a very sweet voice, which people like to hear. It's your duty to use it and give them pleasure." So Kiri would do as she was told, and would sing Maori or English songs to the visitors, as if that were just what she really wanted to do.

"Tom," said Nell to her husband one day, "Kiri has a very good singing voice."

"Yes," agreed Tom.

"We'll have to move," said Nell. "We'll have to move to a bigger place—to a city like Auckland, so that she can have singing lessons from a good teacher."

"Mm." Tom didn't want to move, but he knew that Nell was right. Kiri did have a very good voice, and they would have to go to a big town for her sake.

Kiri didn't want to move either. She didn't want to leave her home or her friends, and she was not all that keen to take singing lessons. But Nell was certain that the family must go, so when Kiri was twelve, the three of them started a new life in Auckland.

There was a good convent there, where Kiri went to school. The singing teacher was a nun, Sister Mary Leo, who had a music room in the grounds. As soon as she heard Kiri sing, she knew that her voice was very special, and she

agreed to give her two lessons a week. She found though, that Kiri liked to sing easy, popular songs and the latest hits. Sister Mary felt that this was rather a waste for such a good voice. She knew that if Kiri worked hard and could go abroad to be trained when she was older, she could become an opera singer, probably a *famous* opera singer.

Nell also had great hopes for her daughter, but Kiri herself wasn't worried by such dreams. She was quite happy to leave school at sixteen, and take an ordinary job. She had a lot of friends and a lot of fun. Nell, however, made her go on taking lessons with Sister Mary, and sometimes Kiri agreed to go in for a singing competition.

There were quite a lot of singing competitions, and Kiri began to win one after another. Then she was often asked to sing at concerts, so that soon she became well known in New Zealand. She had a warm, friendly manner on stage, and everyone loved her. She was very happy, and was quite content with life as it was.

But Nell and Sister Mary wanted her to be trained for opera so that many more people would be able to hear and enjoy her voice. So at last, when Kiri was twenty-two, she went to the

London Opera Centre for training.

Nell was going to travel with her and help her to settle down, but Tom would have to stay at home. Before Kiri left, he gave her a pendant for a present. It was a small fish carved from New Zealand greenstone. It was a Maori symbol, and Kiri put it round her neck and wore it always.

★ ★ ★ ★ ★ ★

So, as time went on, the small, homeless baby, adopted in New Zealand, became a famous opera singer. It would take too long to tell of all her operas and concerts, but one very special event took place in nineteen-eighty-one. Kiri had been singing in Paris, when her agent phoned her from London.

"Kiri," he said, "Charles wants you to sing at his wedding."

"Charles?" replied Kiri. "I don't know anyone called Charles."

"Prince Charles," said her agent.

Prince Charles! Kiri could hardly believe it,

but that summer, when Prince Charles married Lady Diana Spencer in St Paul's Cathedral, Kiri was there. Her voice, strong, beautiful, clear as a bell, rang out to every corner of the packed church. It also reached the ears of six hundred *million* people listening on radio and television across the world.

Long ago, Nell and Tom had looked at the little baby girl, and had said,

"We'll call her Kiri."

Kiri was a Maori word for "bell". It had been a good name to choose.

The information for this story is taken from the book, *Kiri Te Kanawa,* by David Fingleton, published by Collins.

Kiri Te Kanawa singing at the wedding of
Prince Charles and Lady Diana Spencer in
St Paul's Cathedral, 29 July 1981.

The Boy who Loved Ships

Long, long ago, an old and broken ship floated at the river's edge beside the dockyard. Once it had been a warship, with great white sails blowing in the wind and shining cannon fixed upon the deck. But now its sailing days were over, and it was used as a home for Francis and his family.

Francis was a cheerful, friendly boy with curly brown hair, and eyes as grey as the sea. His father was a poor man, a preacher, who read services and prayers to the sailors whose ships were in the dock.

His mother must often have wished for a real house. But even an old ship was better than nothing. So she tied her clothes line to a broken mast, and hung the washing across the deck. She wedged the baby's cradle behind a stand where a cannon had been, and she went on with her work like anyone else.

Francis and his brothers and sisters lived and played and slept on the warship, always swaying up and down a little on the ripples, always hearing the sound of water lapping against the wooden sides. Everywhere they looked, they saw ships and sails and masts. Some of the ships came to the river to be mended. Some had been left there because they were too old to be used any more, but every week there were some that spread their sails and sailed down the river to the sea.

Then there were the sailors always coming and going, always full of wonderful stories that Francis loved to hear—stories of treasure and pirates, and battles with Spanish ships—stories of wild animals and strange people in lands far, far away.

So although Mother wanted a real house, and Father was too poor to buy one, Francis was perfectly happy. And of course he could hardly help growing up to love ships.

While he was still a boy, he joined a small sailing ship. He had to work very hard in all sorts of weather. But he liked the life; and the Captain grew so fond of him that when he died, he left the ship to Francis. So Francis became the Captain of his own ship—and then his adventures began.

There are many stories of Francis Drake when he was a man, but here is just one of them, the story of the Great Armada.

The Great Armada was a fleet of ships belonging to the King of Spain. They were the largest ships that had ever been built. They looked almost like castles floating on the sea, with great sails puffing out in the wind, and guns and cannon set upon the decks. There they were in the ports of Spain, waiting to sail across the sea to attack England.

Everyone in England knew that the Armada would be coming soon. Soldiers kept watch upon the cliffs, ready to give the signal as soon as the Spanish ships appeared. The English navy was ready in the port of Plymouth. The English sailors were waiting for the battle.

In the towns and the villages and the country lanes, people all seemed to talk about the same thing.

"I wonder when the Great Armada will come," they said to each other.

"The sooner the better," said some. "We'll drive it away quickly enough with Francis Drake to command our ships."

Francis Drake by that time was the most famous sailor in England. He had been the first Englishman to sail round the world. He had fought in many battles. He had even led English ships into the ports of Spain, and sunk some of the Spanish ships. So everyone looked to Francis Drake to save the country when the Great Armada came.

But days and weeks went by, and the Armada didn't come. The soldiers watched upon the cliffs. The English navy waited in the port.

Days, weeks and months went by, and still the Great Armada didn't come. Still the soldiers watched upon the cliffs. Still the navy waited in the port.

Weeks, months and even a year went by, and still the Great Armada didn't come. Still the soldiers watched upon the cliffs. Still the navy waited in the port.

Then at last one sunny day in July, a message came from one of the watchmen, and a soldier ran up to the grassy cliff top where Drake was playing bowls with some of his men.

"Sir," said the soldier, "the Great Armada is in sight."

Drake stopped with the wooden ball in his hand. He knew that wind and tide were against him, and that he wouldn't be able to get the English ships out of port until night. He knew that if his men worried and hurried, they might spoil everything. So he said calmly,

"We have time to finish our game, and beat the Spaniards too."

Then he rolled the ball along the grass and went on with the game.

That night, when the tide had turned, Francis Drake led the navy out of port. The sails strained and flapped in the wind, and the air was full of rain and mist. But at last the ships were all out, and the two fleets faced each other across the dark sea—the Armada, great and mighty, and the daring little English ships.

Next day the battle started, and for weeks the sky was grey with smoke; and guns boomed out

across the sea. At night dim lanterns glowed, and English boats, with muffled oars, crept about, setting fireships loose among the enemy. Red flames burst in the darkness, and all the sky was tinged with the glow of fire. The mighty ships of the Great Armada were sinking, or burning, or trying to escape.

The Spaniards were beaten, and all they could hope to do now, was to get back to Spain with the ships that were left. So, with Drake and the English sailing after them, and a sudden

mighty wind scattering them, the ships were blown along the rocky coast, and the Great Armada was broken and beaten at last.

*   *   *   *   *   *

Long, long ago, an old broken ship rotted away at the river's edge, beside the dockyard. Once it had been a warship, with great white sails blowing in the wind, and shining cannon fixed upon the deck. Once it had been the home of Francis Drake, the boy who loved ships.

Prairie Fire

"First!" shouted Terry, scrambling on to a flat rock, and looking very pleased with himself.

"Second!" laughed Linda, climbing up more slowly, and sitting down beside him.

Linda was eight, but Terry was only four, so it had been quite a long walk for him, from the farm to the hilltop.

It wasn't really a hilltop. It was just a patch on the prairie where the ground rose a little, and where there were a few rocks and a twisted willow tree, but the children always called it the hilltop. They liked to sit there on summer days, and look out across the great, wide prairie of America.

They were out of breath now, so they sat for a while without speaking. Terry looked down at the wooden farmhouse in the distance, and at the fields of corn glowing golden in the sun. Linda looked down at a small broken hut half-way between the farm and the hilltop. Once an old man had lived there on a tiny farm, but he had left it long ago. His farm and his pathway were overgrown with long grass now, and only the broken hut and a well, covered with boards, showed that anyone had ever lived there.

"It's quite windy up here," said Linda after a while. "Look at the grass blowing."

Terry wasn't listening. He was twisting himself round on the rock so that he could see the great stretch of land behind them.

"Look!" he said suddenly. Linda turned and looked the way he was pointing.

"Oh!" she murmured in delight. "What a beautiful sunset!"

They both sat in silence gazing at the beauty of the sky. Overhead it was a deep, deep blue, but where it seemed to touch the prairie, it was a vivid, flaming red.

At that moment there was a rustle in the grass, and a prairie dog ran past.

"Prairie dog," whispered Terry, pulling at Linda's arm. "And another! Look."

Linda counted in surprise as six more prairie dogs sped by. At the same time a bird rose with a loud cry and a noisy flutter of wings. The prairie seemed suddenly to be alive with little animals that lived in the grass or burrowed in the earth. Round the hilltop they hurried, and on through the grass—all running, running, running.

"I'm frightened," said Terry, scrambling down from the rock. "I want to go home."

Linda was frightened as well, for she knew all at once why the animals were running. She

knew too that the sky was not red with the sunset. It was much too early in the afternoon for a sunset. The red glow in the sky was the glow of a prairie fire, and the wind was blowing it towards them.

"We must run," said Linda, taking hold of Terry's hand, and climbing down from the hilltop. "It's a prairie fire!" As she spoke, she saw flames rising in the distance, and she felt the pricking of smoke in her eyes.

With Terry panting along beside her, she hurried down the footpath. There had been no rain for weeks. The fire would spread like the wind among the dry grass.

"The farm will be all right," thought Linda, "because Father has dug wide ditches all the way round. So Mother and Father will be safe. I think we've plenty of time to get home really, but I wish Terry could run a little faster."

So the tiny animals in the grass ran, and the prairie dogs ran, and behind them, panting and stumbling, ran Linda and Terry. And behind *them*, crackling in the long grass, flaming in the wind, came the prairie fire—nearer and nearer.

"Run, Terry, run!" cried Linda. Terry was so small and he ran so slowly.

The animals and the dogs ran far from sight. A crowd of birds screamed overhead. The fire spread blazing among the grass. It blew with the wind until all the earth seemed afire.

Terry was so small, his legs were short and fat and his steps were slow. Linda almost dragged him along.

"Run, Terry, run!" she begged.

She hardly dared to turn her head now, for the hilltop was in flames and the fire was close behind her. If only Terry could run faster! If only he could run just a little faster!

In front of her, she saw the old hut. That was exactly half-way between the hilltop and the farm. Only half-way.

Linda knew that however fast they ran now, they would never reach home in time. The fire was almost upon them. What could she do to save Terry and herself? It was useless to go into the broken hut. In a few moments it would become a blazing prison. What could she do?

Suddenly she thought of the old well. It had an iron ladder inside it. She had heard Father say so. She must pull away the boards and take Terry down the well!

"This way," she said, leaving the footpath and running towards the hut. There at the side of it was the well, half covered with boards. The boards were loose. That was lucky. They had been loose for years. In fact Father had said often that he would remove them and fill the well with earth.

Afraid that Terry might fall over the edge, Linda held him with one hand, and pulled away boards with the other. She pulled away one—two, but she couldn't see the iron ladder.

The hilltop was now burnt and dry, and the twisted willow held blackened arms to the glowing sky. All the grass was ablaze. The flames crept nearer, nearer. Linda felt the hot breath of the fire in her face. Perhaps she would not be in time. Perhaps the ladder had gone.

Then, just in time, she found it.

"Quick!" she cried, and holding Terry with one hand, she climbed over the edge of the well, and put her foot on the shaky, iron ladder.

This was too much for Terry. He had run till he was tired. He was small and frightened. There was a great wall of fire around him, and now Linda was taking him down this deep, dark well! It was too much to bear. He opened his mouth and screamed!

Somehow Linda made him put his feet on the iron rungs, and together they went down into the darkness. There was no water in the well, but it felt damp and cold, and there was a strange, strong smell about it.

"Come on, Terry," said Linda bravely. "It won't be for long." And with one hand holding the ladder, and one hand clutching her little brother, she led the way down into the darkness.

★ ★ ★ ★ ★ ★

Now that afternoon Mother was sitting

indoors with a pile of mending beside her. She patched a frock of Linda's and darned a sock of Terry's. Then, because she was so tired, she closed her eyes and fell asleep in her chair. So she knew nothing of the prairie fire until Father came hurrying in from the farm.

"Prairie fire," he said quickly. "Are the children indoors!"

"Yes," said Mother, waking suddenly, and not understanding what he had said. She rubbed her eyes and looked up at Father. Then she said,

"No, no. They went for a walk to the hilltop." She jumped up and ran to the door, dropping scissors and a ball of wool.

"Oh!" she cried, for all around, outside the farm ditches, the prairie was on fire! The flames crackled in the dry grass and blew with the wind. The distant hilltop was burnt and dry, and the twisted willow held blackened arms to the glowing sky.

"Oh!" said Mother again. She and Father

were thinking the same thoughts. Out there, somewhere in the burning grass, were Linda and Terry.

"We mustn't give up hope," said Father. "Be brave. They'll find a safe spot somewhere."

Silently they waited. Swiftly the fire passed on its burning way, leaving the farm like a green and golden island in a great stretch of blackened earth.

Then Mother and Father rode out on their horses to look for the children. The horses gave cries of fear and pain as their hooves trod the hot earth.

"Come on, come on," said Father, urging them forward.

In fear and hope they rode over the blackened grass. Smoke pricked their eyes and hurt their throats.

"On, on!" cried Father to the horses.

Soon they came to the place where the hut had been.

"The children may have run to the hut,"

whispered Mother, frightened.

"I hope not," murmured Father, for the hut, now, was just a pile of charred wood lying on the ground, still in flames.

Mother pulled at her horse and brought him to a standstill. Sadly she gazed at the red sky and the black earth. She was thinking about Terry and Linda.

Father's horse stood still too. Father was thinking the same thoughts.

Then suddenly there was a sound! It sounded like voices singing—softly and far away. But it couldn't be. Of course it couldn't be.

Mother looked at Father. Father looked at Mother.

Then it came again. It was the sound of muffled voices, getting louder and clearer. They were singing cheerfully.

"Ding dong dell. Pussy's in the well," they sang.

And at that moment two tousled heads and grubby faces appeared at the top of the well.

"Linda! Terry!" cried Mother.

"Linda! Terry!" cried Father.

★ ★ ★ ★ ★ ★

In a few minutes the horses were galloping back over the burnt grass to the farm. On one horse rode Mother and Terry. Terry said nothing. He cuddled up against her and went straight to sleep.

On the other horse rode Father and Linda.

"Terry was frightened," explained Linda. "So I told him stories, and then I made him sing with me. It was a good idea singing 'Ding dong dell,' wasn't it?"

"A very good idea," said Father.

"It was a good idea going down the well, wasn't it?" went on Linda.

Father gazed at the red sky and the charred earth. He looked back a moment at the burnt hilltop and the twisted willow holding out its blackened arms. Then he said softly,

"It was a wonderful idea, Linda—a *wonderful* idea!"

The Olympic Games

The Greeks of ancient times thought it was very important to be fit and healthy. They loved athletics and they also loved to compete with one another; so all over Greece they held regular athletic festivals.

The most important of these were the Olympic Games. They were held every four years at Olympia in the south-west of Greece. This was the home of Zeus, the king of the Greek gods, and the games were held in his honour.

Olympia was a beautiful fertile plain lying between two rivers and surrounded by low hills. In it there were temples, statues, a stadium for the athletic competitions, a gymnasium and other fine buildings.

From all over the Greek world people came to Olympia to compete in the games or to watch them.

In the scorching heat of midsummer the

athletes competed in discus and spear throwing, running, wrestling, boxing, chariot racing and other sports. But, unlike today, there were no team games.

The contests went on for five days. On the last day of the games, the winners went to the

The ruins of the Temple of Zeus at Olympia.

Temple of Zeus and thanked the god for their victory. Then they went home with their prizes and were treated like heroes.

The Games were held every four years for more than a thousand years. Then, in A.D. 393, they were banned. By that time, Greece had become part of the Roman Empire and the Christian faith had taken the place of the old Greek gods.

So the Temple of Zeus and the other buildings stood empty and unused. Some of the statues were taken away and some buildings were destroyed. Then one of the rivers overflowed its banks and covered the site with a thick layer of mud.

★ ★ ★ ★ ★ ★

For 1400 years Olympia lay buried. Then archaeologists digging at the site found the remains of the ancient Temple of Zeus. This interesting discovery made people think about reviving the idea of the Olympic Games.

The first modern Olympic Games were held in Athens in 1896 and, except in time of war, they have been held every four years ever since then.

The Olympic Games of olden times were only for the people of Greece. But the modern Olympics are open to all nations. From the start they have been held in a different country each time. The countries that have been hosts to the modern Olympics are: France, the United Kingdom, Sweden, the Netherlands, the USA, Germany, Finland, Australia, Italy, Japan, Mexico, Canada and the USSR.

The modern Olympic Games now have a very interesting history of their own. At the London games of 1908, the marathon of 26 miles was lengthened by another 385 yards. This was done so that the runners going round the track at the Wembley Stadium would finish right in front of the royal box! The standard length of the marathon was later fixed at 26 miles 385 yards (42.195 kilometres).

Until the Stockholm Games of 1912, you could enter without being part of a national team. This is now impossible. At Stockholm, a Finnish runner took three gold medals and started the tradition of Finnish excellence in middle and long distance running.

For a long time, Americans have excelled in the swimming events, and the Paris Games of 1924 produced Johnny Weismuller, who won five gold medals. He later became famous as Tarzan in the cinema.

Women were not allowed to take part in the track and field events until 1928, in Amsterdam. Before that time athletics were not thought to be suitable for women!

In 1936, the famous American athlete, Jesse Owen, made a record long jump of 26 feet $5\frac{1}{4}$ inches. This record stood until 1960 when it was broken by another American athlete. Then in 1968 in Mexico City, a huge leap of 29 feet $2\frac{1}{2}$ inches (8.90 metres) was made by Bob Beamon, also from the USA.

(*Left*) The opening ceremony at the 1980 Olympic Games in Moscow. The torch-bearer on his way to light the Olympic flame. (*Above*) The Olympic flame burning at the 1980 Winter Olympic at Lake Placid, USA.

The Games are opened by lighting the Olympic flame with a torch carried all the way from Olympia in Greece. This tradition started in 1936, at the Berlin Games. The torch is lit at Olympia by means of the sun and a powerful magnifying glass. Then a team of runners carry the flame to wherever the Games are to be held.

The pole vault event, Moscow Olympics, 1980.

The athletes of the 1896 Games would be amazed to see how some sports have developed. Such things as modern running tracks, better training and improved methods have broken records in every sport again and again. Each Olympiad (there are still four years between the Games) produces fresh talent, new world records and the promise of another exciting display of athletic skill. It is now a major sporting event, which interests people all over the world. Thanks to satellite television, people can watch the events as they are taking place thousands of miles away.

But the spirit of the Games has not changed. They bring together people from many different countries and ways of life. The Olympic Games are an occasion when nations can put aside their differences and enjoy sport in the same way as the ancient Greeks. As the founder of the modern Olympics said, "The important thing in the Olympic Games is not winning, but taking part."

Daley Thompson

Francis Daley Thompson was born in Notting Hill, West London on the thirtieth of July 1958. His father was Nigerian and his mother Scottish. Their son was to become one of the world's greatest athletes.

When Daley was three years old he was sent to a nursery school. It was not a success. His mother was asked to take him away from the school because he was always fighting—and fighting to win.

When he was seven, Daley was sent to a boarding school in Sussex. He was encouraged to take an interest in games and soon sport was taking up most of his time. His first love was football and he became a very good player, so good in fact that later he had trials for two league clubs—Fulham and Chelsea. It seemed that he might become a professional footballer.

But then he became interested in athletics. His headmaster sent him to join a local athletics club, Haywards Heath Harriers. He soon became a success as a sprinter and jumper.

Daley's teenage years, however, brought problems. His parents had separated when he was eight and when he was thirteen his father died. At the age of sixteen he decided to make athletics his career. But his mother wanted him to settle in a safe job. Daley and his mother had many arguments and finally he left home and went to live with his Aunt Doreen.

There were more problems to come. In 1974

he took part in the English Schools Championships at Shrewsbury. Running in the 200 metres, Daley could only come fourth. Later he took part in the AAA Junior Championships and was beaten. He hated being a loser and thought of leaving athletics for football.

Then he met Bob Mortimer, an official of another athletics club, Essex Beagles. Bob encouraged Daley to continue in athletics and became his first club coach.

Two things kept Daley Thompson in athletics. The first was his own courage and determination to be successful. The second was Bob Mortimer. As well as being Daley's coach, he was now a close friend. He knew Daley better than anyone else. He could see that Daley had a natural ability in athletics, and that he had a strong, muscular build. Daley is 1.87 metres tall and weighs around 85.75 kilograms.

Bob Mortimer asked Daley to leave sprinting and train for the decathlon (ten events). Daley agreed, and he began to train hard. He vowed that the three athletes who had beaten him in Shrewsbury would never beat him again. They never did.

From the time he began training, there was no doubt in Daley's mind about his future. He was going to be a champion decathlete, even if it took years of hard work. And at last, in July 1980, he achieved his ambition. At the Moscow Olympic games he stood proudly on the winners' platform while the gold medal was hung round his neck. Aunt Doreen was there to see him become the decathlon champion of the world.

Winning the decathlon is never easy. There are ten events, spread over two days of competition. They are always run in the same order. The events of the first day are the 100 metres, long jump, shot, high jump and 400 metres. On the second day they are the 110 metres hurdles, discus, pole vault, javelin and 1500 metres.

Points are given for each event, and then added together. Daley's total of 8495 points was the highest ever recorded.

After the race Daley said he had never thought of losing. Not everyone liked Daley when he spoke like this. One Australian athlete called him "a pain in the neck". But to his coach he was a lively, talkative person with simple tastes. Although he would drink champagne to celebrate winning a race, Daley's favourite foods were chocolate, toast and marmalade.

Unless he had done his best, even in training, Daley wasn't happy. In the early days of training for the decathlon, he'd improved his pole vault from 2.75 metres to 3.80 metres. His aim was to clear 3.90 metres. Only then would he think of himself as a real vaulter. When he took part in the 1980 Olympic games decathlon, he cleared 4.70 metres, and felt he could vault

Throwing the javelin. World Athletics Championships, Helsinki, 1983.

even higher. He was determined to be the most successful decathlete of all time.

For a few weeks after the Olympic games Daley was able to relax. He stopped training, and spent his time with his friends, talking and eating a lot. But soon he was restless, and began training again. Athletics were his life.

Once he was the Olympic champion, Daley dreamt of becoming the decathlon champion at the European games and the Commonwealth games in 1982. This meant another two years of hard work. He trained eight hours a day, working six or even seven days a week.

His day began about 10 a.m. with a twenty minute run in Wimbledon, where he lived with his Aunt Doreen. Next he practised throwing the discus. In the afternoon he drove his car into London, and trained there for the hurdles, javelin and long jump. In the evening he practised the sprints, high jump and pole vault, finishing at about 9 p.m. Then Daley, and some of his friends who trained with him, would visit

McDonald's for hamburgers and Coke. The next morning he began the training programme again.

During his training Daley suffered from the usual minor injuries that athletes can expect. These were mainly strains and pulled muscles. Daley said that he ached all the time. Yet, even if he wasn't feeling well, he talked himself into performing well. "If I have a cold, I won't even sneeze," he said.

But in July 1982 Daley had a more serious injury. His pole snapped during a competition. The jagged end tore his elbow, and he wasn't able to train for three weeks. Even after this accident, Daley won the pole vault in the Welsh games in August.

Although he was the Olympic champion, Daley didn't win every decathlon competition. In the summer of 1982 he was beaten by Jurgen Hingsen of West Germany. Hingsen scored a record 8723 points. Coming second was of no use to Daley Thompson.

The next month, September, Daley was to meet Jurgen Hingsen again at the European games in Athens. Daley wanted the record back.

The games began badly for Daley. At the end of the first day of the decathlon he was more than 100 points behind his own record. Daley told his friends not to expect too much. It looked as though Hingsen would win the gold medal and Daley the silver medal.

The second day began with the hurdles. Daley won his heat. Hingsen came third. In the discus event, Daley was behind Hingsen until the third throw. With a great effort, Daley made his best ever throw. He now had a real chance of winning the decathlon.

Hingsen's best event in the decathlon was usually the javelin, but again Daley beat him. That only left the final event, the 1500 metres.

The 1500 metres race is one the decathletes dislike. They are usually big and heavily

The 1500 metres race, World Athletics Championships, Helsinki, 1983.

muscled, so running this distance is never easy for them. Also, the weather was very hot in Athens, and the athletes were already tired. As soon as the starting gun was fired, Hingsen was off and in the lead. He led until the last lap. Only then was Daley Thompson able to pass him, winning the race in a spectacular 4 minutes 23.71 seconds. He had broken the world decathlon record by 20 points, with a score of 8743.

Afterwards, Daley told how much he had pushed himself to get through the 1500 metres race. "I had to think of things to make myself angry, or I wouldn't have kept going. I thought I wasn't going to make the last lap. When I finished I couldn't even read the time clock. I was so dizzy I couldn't see clearly."

But he had won. The newspapers called him the greatest ever decathlete. . . . the man who could run, jump, throw and vault better than anyone in history.

So part of Daley's dream had come true. He

had achieved a unique distinction. He was the first decathlete to hold the world record and the Olympic, European and Commonwealth titles at the same time.

In October 1982, he wanted to defend his Commonwealth title. Before the games began in Brisbane, Australia, Daley disappointed the English team. Because of his success in Athens, he was invited to carry the flag in the opening parade. He refused the invitation and wouldn't give a reason. Phillip Hubble, the Olympic and European swimming silver medallist, carried the flag instead of Daley.

In Brisbane, the weather was hot and damp. It was only after the games ended that a thunderstorm cleared the air. It was exhausting for the decathletes, who had to take part in ten events. But nothing could stop Daley Thompson. Only one month after the European games, he repeated his success and kept his Commonwealth title. At the age of twenty-five he had achieved his major ambition to hold all three titles—the Olympic, European and Commonwealth—at the same time.

In the autumn of 1982 the British Athletics Writers' Association voted Daley Thompson the "Athlete of the Year". It was a triumphant end to Daley's most successful year.

But the man who has been called Britain's most successful athlete was still looking to the future. He had many more medals to win.

"I'd like to earn a million," says Daley Thompson, "but I'm an athlete first and foremost."

Anne B. English